The Newlywed

Handbook

The Newlywed Handbook

Oscar & Crystal Jones

DESTINY HOUSE PUBLISHING LLC

The Newlywed Handbook
Published by Destiny House Publishing LLC

Copyright ©2010 Oscar & Crystal Jones
ISBN:1452847126

Original printing May 2010

**Cover design and Publication Layout:
Destiny House Publishing LLC**

**Editing: Write Away
www.writeaway.biz**

Printed in the United States of America

**For information:
Destiny House Publishing LLC
www.destinyhousepublishing.com
P.O. Box 19774
Detroit, MI 48219
888-890-9455**

Acknowledgment
and
Dedication

We humbly acknowledge the One from whom we obtained the knowledge and wisdom to write this book. If there is any glory or any praise, it must go to Him. We know nothing in and of ourselves. He gave us a picture of the perfect marriage to copy. Thank you, Lord Jesus.

This book is dedicated to our "single" children, Kyria, Charity, LaTina, and Christopher. It is our prayer that you will be selective and prayerful in choosing to whom you will say, "I Do". It's an important decision and should not be entered into lightly.

We also dedicate this book to our married children Jake & Keila Allen and all of our mentees: Some are single and others who have been married 10 years or less:

Jake & Keila Allen
Michelle Bailey
Bianca Bronson
Bobbie Jean Crawford
Darnell & Ra'sheedah Deboes
Anthony McCray
T'Vo & LaQuitia Robinson
Rochelle Smith

Table of Contents

How to Use This Handbook

This handbook has 11 sections. It is intended to be a 11-week study course. Plan to take one week for each section. This handbook has 2 components: the main section and the break-out sections. We advise couples to read through the main sections of each chapter and then answer the questions in the break-out sections. The break-out section allows the husband and wife to answer each question separately from his/her own ideas and experiences. It is best after you have completed the break-out section, to come back together and discuss your answers. It will be enlightening to see each other's responses.

We estimate that each section will take 1 hour to 1 ½ hours to complete. Be focused on your readings. Don't rush through the material. Be honest and revealing in answering the material and with the discussion. You want to get the most out of the study as possible and thereby allowing your marriage to flourish.

Chapter 6 has a Parent Project. This will take a little more time to complete. Please do not skip over this project. It is an important step in the process. Chapter 9, Money Matters section, will also take a little longer to complete. There is a joint section that must be completed after the individual sections.

At the end of the book we have compiled a list of the 10 Commandments of Marriage. Take time to go over these. It's sort of an at-a-glance marriage guide. Don't be afraid to tear it out of the book and post it on the refrigerator. Or post it in a place that you will see everyday.

At the very end, there is also a section devoted to commonly asked questions. We pray that you will find this to be a helpful resource.

Introduction

This workbook was designed to help those looking to marry as well as those who have been married 10 years or less. But understand the fact that the principles within these pages can be applied to all marriages, no matter how old. We should be ever learning how to please God and our spouses. Proverbs 4:4 says, *Get wisdom, get understanding forget it not: neither decline from the words of my mouth; forsake her not and she shall preserve thee, love her and she shall keep thee.*

Many marriages have ended tragically, because when troubles appeared they simply just didn't know what else to do. Well, it is our hope that this book will answer those questions. Life puts many demands on marriages: work deadlines, children, health issues, finances, extended relationships, etc. Through this book, couples will learn how to thrive in their marriage and minimize the pressures.

The enemy hates marriage. It is the reflective glory of God in the earth. *John 10:10 reads, "The thief cometh not but for to steal, kill, and destroy: I am come that they might have life, and that they might have it more abundantly."* So he will do whatever possible to destroy your marriage. Because we are not ignorant of his schemes, we can put safeguards around our union to keep the evil one out.

Prayerfully, we expect that this book will be a valuable resource to you as you lay a solid foundation in your life together as a married couple. The foundation is the strongest part of any building, when it is formed properly.

Let us begin by building on a foundation of Jesus Christ. *I Corinthians 3:11 For other foundation can no man lay than that is laid, which is Jesus Christ.* Every healthy marriage must be built on Him. Matthew 7:24, 25 *Therefore whosoever heareth these sayings of mine, and doeth them, I will liken him unto a wise man, which builds his house upon a rock: and the rain descended, and the floods came, and the wind blew, and beat upon that house; and it fell not: for it was founded upon a rock.* The solid rock of God's word will keep your house/marriage from crumbling.

If you don't know the Lord, it is important that you develop a love relationship with Him. You can start by giving him sole reign over your life. God loves you and wants to be involved in every aspect of your life. You must invite Him in. Recognizing that you need Jesus is the first step toward a successful relationship. And repenting or turning from our old lifestyle is step two. The third step is to get planted in a Bible believing church where you can learn and grow in the Word. You will find that a life in Christ is essential in living a successful life and building thriving relationships.

> *If you confess with your mouth the Lord Jesus and believe in your heart that God has raised Him from the dead thou shalt be saved. Romans 10:9*

Pray this simple prayer:

I confess that I am a sinner and that I can do nothing in my own strength. Lord, Jesus, you are the only begotten Son of the Father. I recognize that you died for my sins. And I accept the work that you did on the cross. Forgive me for my sins. Come and live in my heart forever. In Jesus' name I pray, Amen.

Chapter 1
Prescription for a Good Marriage

God's original intent for marriage was that the union was to be enjoyed. He told Adam to name the animals. He was creating a desire in Adam for companionship. Eve was never an afterthought. God knew that He would create Eve from the beginning, because it was not good for Adam to not have an Eve. God had a surprise for Adam, an amazing gift. He awakened Adam to this creature of beauty. And He told Adam to become one with her. Enjoy her. All through scripture, he reminds man to enjoy the wife of his youth. Jesus said that I came that you might have life and that more abundantly. Marriage was never meant to be looked at with drudgery and disdain. God intended for us to have the time of our lives.

Unfortunately, marriage isn't always a joyful experience. What we have failed to realize is that the joyful side of marriage must be done intentionally. It won't just happen on its own. We must purposely seize the life that God intended. Otherwise we will either be sour and bitter like many marriages that we've seen; or we just won't make it as evidenced by the soaring divorce rate.

How do we do it on purpose? There are certain things that are necessary in the recipe for a healthy marriage. We have listed those basic ingredients. We hope that you will institute them in your own relationship and celebrate married

#1 Keep Covenant

Never threaten to divorce one another. Make a pact that you won't ever speak the word in your home. The Word of God speaks clearly: "'I hate divorce," says the Lord God of Israel" (NIV/Malachi 2:16). We cannot embrace something that God says that He hates! Let us *not* keep this as a side option, in case our mates don't "act right". God's idea was that marriage would last for an entire lifetime. God never divorces the church, even though she has not always been faithful to him. The marriage covenant is holy and binding. The scripture makes it clear that marriage is to be broken only by death.

The key to a successful marriage is eliminating a failed marriage as an option. When challenges arise, you must be willing to work through them. If both parties commit to do everything to make the marriage work, your marriage can only be successful. We must accept the teachings of the Word of God rather than the false philosophies of this world's system.

The world promotes the concept that, if a marriage doesn't work out, we can always get a divorce and move on. Challenge the status quo. There really is nothing too hard for our God.

As believers, we are called to accept God's view of marriage and reject the thinking of the world, which takes marriage so lightly. It is not conducive to your marriage to consider divorce or to talk about it. It is much better to dwell on the hope of getting through difficult seasons. A wounded marriage can be healed. We know that Jesus is our Chief Healer. And nothing is beyond his power.

For the Lord, the God of Israel says that he hateth putting away (divorce). Malachi 2:16

#2 Date Your Mate

Couples should institute a date night, once a week. While this may sound easy, it will be very challenging to keep. Date night is an important element to a healthy relationship. We encourage you to not look at date night as a luxury or as an option. Date night is a necessity. If your perspective is that dating is indispensable, you will most likely press to keep up with it. You will be challenged in keeping up with a date night. But remember, it is very important. You will be hard pressed to find a couple headed for divorce court that is dating each other on a regular basis.

Your date nights should be fun and exciting. They don't have to be lavish or expensive. It is a time to enjoy one another. You could do something simple like have a picnic in the living room by the fireplace. Dream about your future together. Be creative. Plan a romantic getaway. Laugh as you go through old photos. The purpose of date night is to make pleasant memories. It is a time to reconnect with your spouse regularly. You keep the home fire burning by dating your spouse. (You will find dating ideas at the end of this chapter).

Let thy fountain be blessed and rejoice with the wife of thy youth. Proverbs 5:16

#3 Husband-Wife meetings

Once a week, set aside some quality time to talk about issues that hang heavy on your hearts; or issues that could turn sour if not properly handled. This is what we call husband-wife meetings or hammer meetings. It's a friendly fireside chat designed to work the bugs out of your relationship.

The agenda should be set ahead of time. The meeting should last no more than two hours. The purpose of hammer meetings or husband-wife meetings is to avoid handling difficult issues on a daily basis. It is not wise to discuss every negative issue that comes up in marriage. You could find yourself arguing everyday. Save those worth dealing with for your hammer meetings. (More on this at the end of the chapter).

Submitting yourselves one to another in the fear of God. Ephesians 5:21

#4 Get-Away

Couples should get away from the busyness of their lives. Go to a hotel or bed and breakfast once every quarter. If this is not possible, getaway at least once a year, until you can work your way up to once quarterly. This, too, is not an option, but a necessity. If you lose the romance of your relationship, it's hard to enjoy one another. Stay connected.

Come, my beloved, let us go forth into the field; let us lodge in the villages. Let us get up early to the vineyards; let us see if the vine flourish, whether the tender grape appear, and the pomegranates bud forth: there will I give thee my loves. Song of Solomon 7:11-12

#5 Read, Learn and Listen

Couples should attend at least one marriage conference per year. And take part of marriage gatherings/fellowships as often as possible. It helps to bring understanding to the unique dynamic of the marriage relationship. Marriage is a living entity. It needs to be cultivated and watered.

Read the Bible and other books on marriage. Work through a couples' devotional. Glean from others' experience and wisdom. We do not have to suffer through everything ourselves. Experience is not the best teacher; but it is often the hardest teacher.

Couples are able to learn about the different seasons of marriage and become skilled at how to approach those seasons. It also helps when a couple experiences a rough patch in their union to see that their situation is not unique. Every marriage will have some hard places to work through. Marriage conferences/retreats help you to avoid some pitfalls and work your way through others.

Through wisdom is a house built; and by understanding it is established: And by knowledge shall the chambers be filled with all precious and pleasant riches.
Proverbs 24:3,4

#6 Prayer

Pray for your marriage. Pray for your spouse. This seems simple enough. However, it is an area that is most neglected by married persons. You will find that prayer is an essential tool in laying a proper foundation for a healthy marriage. Couples should carve out time to pray together regularly. Pray for the marriage. Don't just pray for challenges as they present themselves in your relationships. But pray for preventive health as well. Pray that certain things will not hit your marriage. Pray for each other. This keeps your heart tender toward your spouse. And by all means, pray for yourself.

This will keep you humble and keep you aware of your own frailties and potential to blow it. As we come to God and allow him to show us ourselves, we can become more diligent in working on our relationships. We have included a husband and wife's prayer just to get you started.

A Husband's Prayer

O Lord, I lift up to you the most amazing gift given to me in this life, my precious wife. May I always love her, cherish her, and nourish her.
Forgive me for those times I have neglected her and taken her for granted.

Lord, fill my mouth with praise for her instead of complaints and criticisms. Help me to talk to her when I don't feel like it and share my most intimate feelings with her. Help me to love her like you loved the church, by dying to my own selfish needs and desires. And remind me to always keep her in first position right behind you.

May I never abuse my authority as her head. Teach me how to lovingly lead her back to you and never to myself. May I always pastor her, protect her, and provide for her according to your will.

Lord, this is my wife. You have created her for me. Let my love cover her sins and heal her brokenness. May I encourage her in her own gifts and talents, and never be threatened by her abilities.

As we are on this journey together, may I never leave her feeling alone, but always comforted by my love. And as we look back, may we never regret the journey but enjoy it until we get home.

In Jesus' name I pray. Amen

A Wife's Prayer

O Lord, I lift up to you my love, my friend, and leader. Forgive me Lord for speaking harshly to him. Forgive me for not allowing him to be the man you've called him to be. Forgive me for interfering with his walk and his ministry. Deliver me O Lord from unforgiveness and rashness of words. Help me to be submissive to him, to be quick to hear and slow to speak. Cleanse me from my own flesh, O Lord, that wants to hold grudges and recall the past.

Lord, fill my mouth with pleasant words that will encourage him and lift him up. Let my tongue be filled with the law of kindness. And let me do him good and not evil all the days of my life.

Lord, this is my husband. Let there be no time in his life that I tear him down. Help me, O Lord, to build him up and to walk in holy submission toward him. Teach me how to trust him, how to make him shine, and to love him.

Lord, this is my husband that you've created for me. May I never disrespect him, but honor him. May I never damage his spirit, but encourage him. May I never expect him to meet all of my needs. But may they be met in you. Let my love give him confidence, so that he does safely trust in me. When our journey together is complete, Dear Lord, may he arise up, call me blessed and praise me in the gates.

In Jesus' name, I pray. Amen.

Once you have laid this foundation of prayer, take time to review this chapter. At the end of this chapter, we have listed the Great Dates section as well as the format for the Husband-Wife Meeting. To get the most out of this book, we encourage you to put them to use.

The subsequent chapters will help you build a strong relationship. They will also serve as a marriage resource, when you hit a snag, to come back to the specific chapter and be reminded of how to properly handle each life challenge.

You will also find a helpful Break Out section at the end of each chapter. This handy section was created to give you practice. So take time to answer the questions together and do the homework. It will prove to be quite beneficial.

Great Dates

Often couples get stuck in a routine. Their date night is the same every week. Either they go out to eat, or to the movies, or both. That is the extent of their variety. We encourage you to experiment with things you've never done nor even thought of doing. Break out of the monotony. Keep your marriage fresh and interesting.

Plan a candlelight bath
Go to a carnival or amusement park (indoor or outdoor)
Plan a romantic picnic with all your favorite foods.
Take a walk along the beach or riverfront
Watch the fireworks
Go ice-skating or roller-skating (even if you don't know how)
Go skiing or sledding
Chat by the fireplace
Tour a mansion
Adult Only Game Night (make it interesting)
Go to a museum or cultural center
Take dance lessons
Go bike riding
Go canoeing or paddle boating
Take cooking classes Get tickets to a sporting event (college or professional)
Take a ride through a ritzy neighborhood (pick out your dream house)
Watch the sunset

Are finances a hindrance to a great date? Here are some

Money-saving Tips:

1. Trade babysitting services with another young couple. We did this when our children were young. We had 4 little people at the time. So babysitting costs were not in the budget. Our friends had three. So every other week we would babysit for them and they would reciprocate.
2. It is not necessary that you leave the house for all of your date nights. Maybe every other date night, you could leave the house. On the nights you stay in, power off all cell phones and eliminate all distractions. Park your car in the garage. And plan to a have a romantic picnic in the backyard. Or set up the basement like a café. Be creative.
3. Put younger children to bed. Older children must do an activity in their room. Our children understood every Friday was date night. This meant that they had to watch a movie or read a book and could not disturb mom and dad. This worked pretty well in our household. Tattling was not allowed unless it was an emergency.
4. Empty all your loose change into a container at the end of each day. We averaged $30 to $50 per month in coins. Make this the date night fund.
5. If you live in an area where bottles and cans are recyclable. Save all of your bottles and cans towards your date night fund. Newspapers are also recyclable.
6. Check the newspaper or online for free events in your area. It will surprise you the things that are available. We have found outdoor movies (during the summer), salsa lessons, Christian concerts, and much more.

7. Eat dinner at home and then go out for dessert and coffee/tea.
8. Turn your bedroom into a spa. Get relaxing music. Light candles. Give each other massages.

Some of the ideas we listed in Great Dates, require no money at all. You just need to let those creative juices flow.

Husband-Wife Meetings

The idea of husband-wife meeting is new to a lot of couples. So we have created a form to help bring guidance and direction to the meeting. Remember the purpose is to avoid dealing with negative issues *everyday*. And to bring solutions to issues that arise in the relationship. So husband-wife meeting is to be held once a week. It should never be the same day as date night.

Spend time in prayer and meditation before you put an issue on the list. Follow the Lord's leading. Some issues won't make the list. Others will be delayed before putting them on the list.

There are times when tempers will be so heated that you cannot wait until the meeting to deal with the problem. It is fine to deal with it at the time it arises. But a word of caution: every issue should not be that pressing. You should have enough temperance to be able to wait until the appropriate time to deal with issues.

No meeting should last longer than 1 ½ to 2 hours. ALWAYS pray before starting your husband wife meeting. Pray for oneness. Pray against the spirit of strife and contention.

After you have prayed together, each spouse should acknowledge something that has improved in the relationship. Don't make your spouse feel like nothing he/she does is right. Identify something that he or she has done that blessed you or the family.

Accept the fact, that most likely, you will not complete every issue on your list, every week. That's okay. Any issue(s) left on the table should rollover to the following week. Some issues will work themselves out. You may be one of the few couples who come to a week and have no issues. Take the time to pray and thank God for that week; then dismiss husband-wife meeting.

Hopefully you will learn to activate patience and self-control by waiting until the time for husband-wife meeting to bring up an issue. Patience will also be demonstrated when you pray before adding the issue to the list.

Sample issues that should be brought to the table:
Children's behavior in school or at home
A remark that was made by an in-law
Feelings of neglect
Trust issues
Communication breakdowns
Bills due or overdue
Angry actions

Benefits of conducting successful Husband-Wife Meetings

<u>Wife</u> - She feels affirmed and heard when solutions are implemented. She has a time and place for expressing the issues on her heart. She learns patience and self-control. She doesn't feel harassed or irritated by constant complaining.

<u>Husband</u> - He doesn't feel nagged about negative issues everyday. He feels affirmed in that everything he is doing is not wrong. He learns to listen and become more sensitive. He has a time and place to express the issues on his heart. He, too, learns patience and self-control.

Husband-Wife Meetings

Date: _____

Time: _____ (2 hr limit)

Prayer

Each spouse must highlight 1 thing that has improved or is going right

Topics to be discussed by wife:

_____

_____

Topics to be discussed by husband:

_____

_____

Solutions:

_____

_____

Topics for next week:

_____

_____

_____

Chapter 2
Communication & Conflict Resolution

Every marriage will have conflict. It is unavoidable. You are two individuals who come from different family backgrounds and you have different ideals. At times, these will clash. Don't be alarmed. It is normal for spouses to disagree. The goal is not to be free of conflict but to handle conflict correctly. When conflict is handled correctly, the couple will move closer to becoming one. This is the real work of marriage. You are working on your marriage when you work toward resolving conflict. Often people think that the work of marriage is demonstrated in the good times. Not so. It is demonstrated in difficult times.

A dead zone is created when couples hit a wall in their communication. They can no longer "hear" each other. Each is concerned with making his/her own point or winning the argument. The communication ball has been dropped.

Dead zones are created:

- When we don't get our way
- When we feel we are not being heard
- When our rights are violated
- When we have unmet expectations
- Or when we've been hurt

Couples must work carefully to have healthy communication. This means we need to avoid hitting a dead zone, where communication stops.

Each spouse must decide for him/herself, if the offense even necessitates confronting. It is important to choose your battles wisely or you will find yourself fighting over every little thing. Proverbs 19:11 says, "The discretion of a man deferreth his anger; and it's his glory to pass over a transgression." Simply put, "Smart people know how to hold their tongue; their grandeur is to forgive and forget (Message)." It is not wise to sweat the small stuff. Be selective about which conflict you will address.

If you address every matter that arises, you will have less influence when there is a larger issue that you are facing. Your spouse may begin to tune you out or think, "What's the point? She/He is always upset about something." So be very selective about confrontation. If you live long enough, the matter will resurface later in the relationship when it is a more appropriate time to address: or either it will be resolved.

It is imperative that you continuously examine your motives. What are you aiming to accomplish? Are you trying to retaliate? Are you trying to punish your spouse? Do you want to prove your point? Or are you interested in pursuing peace? Hopefully you are interested in only the latter. The issue is at risk, not your love or relationship. So choose your words wisely. And stay focused on the subject at hand.

Once you have decided that this is one for the hammer meeting, write it down. Then pray about the timing and make sure you have engaged the Father, Son, & Holy Spirit in this. This will help you to avoid a dead zone. Timing is important. You must exercise temperance until the appointed time. God will back you. And you won't be as quick to dip over into the flesh. *He that handleth a matter wisely shall find good: and whoso trusteth in the LORD, happy is he. Proverbs 16:20*

How do I know if we have hit a dead zone?

One or both are…

-Engaging in silent treatment
-Yelling/screaming or name-calling
-Shutting down (pseudo agreement)
-Walking away or withdrawing
-Sarcasm

Dead zone #1 → *The silent treatment* is a battle for control. Often a spouse is withdrawing their conversation, acknowledgment, and acceptance from the relationship. This is a manipulative way of punishing your spouse. It is a prideful response and not useful for conflict resolution or healthy communication. Some couples go days, weeks, months and even years without speaking to one another. God is not pleased with this type of behavior. The scriptures remind us, *"Be ye angry and sin not, let not the sun go down on your anger". Ephesians 5:26*

Dead Zone #2 →*Name calling* is immature and ineffective. Always attack the problem and not the person. For example, it is disrespectful to call your husband lazy because he didn't complete some task that you asked of him. It is equally as dishonoring to call your wife a nag because she continues to bring up the incomplete task.

Accusations never accomplish much. It is the nature of our enemy to accuse. Focus on the incomplete task or the fact that the request is repetitive. Do not criticize your spouse. *A soft answer turns away wrath. But grievous words stir up anger. Proverbs 15:1*

Dead Zone #3 → *Shutting down* is usually a "poor me"

19

response. It is not effective to agree with your spouse for the sake of agreement. Or just because you feel you aren't being heard. Keep talking. Keep praying. Keep trying to get through....for better and for worse. Speak the truth in love (Eph 4:15). Be honest with one another.

Don't pretend or cover up for the sake of a false peace. Lovingly confront issues that could hinder the relationship. You don't want to gloss over an issue and then find many years later that you still have bitterness because something was never honestly handled. At the same time, confront with humility. *And in her tongue is law of kindness. Proverbs 31:6b*

Dead Zone #4 → **Walking away** from your spouse because you refuse to continue to work out the problem is also ineffective. If you need to take a break or a cooling off period, make that plain and clear. But don't withdraw from your spouse or the situation. You are part of the solution. Stay engaged in the process of conflict resolution. *Let us hear the conclusion of the whole matter. Ecclesiastes 12:13*

Dead Zone #5 → **Sarcasm** is ugly and negative. It is bitter ridicule or a cutting remark. You will not have productive problem-solving when sarcasm is present. It shows a lack of respect. Be kind and proactive in working through whatever problems arise. Every couple has conflict. But every couple does not approach conflict in a constructive way. If you come from a sarcastic family, you may find it very natural to be sarcastic. But if you understand that it will eat away at your marriage, you can work at being more sensitive to your spouse. *Let no corrupt communication proceed out of your mouth but that which is good to the use of edifying that it may minister grace unto the hearers. Ephesians 4:29*

Remember your spouse is NOT your enemy. You have one true adversary. He throws the rock and hides his hand. Do not lay the blame at the feet of your one flesh partner. Recognize the enemy for the crafty con that he is. His aim is to divide you. Be smart. Be vigilant. Your adversary walks as a roaring lion seeking whom he may devour. The interesting thing about a roaring lion is that you can hear him. We do not have to be ignorant of his schemes.

It is healthy to consider your contribution to the conflict. Ask yourself the following questions: What role did I play? What pattern or habit of mine contributed to the conflict? How could I have had a better response to the conflict? Could this issue have been avoided by my response?

Resolving Conflict requires forgiveness. Healthy conflict resolution occurs when couples are *willing* to seek and offer forgiveness.

Break Out: Husband

Talk about an issue this week in your husband-wife meeting. Practice conflict resolution.

Below are areas that we are most susceptible to anger.

Discuss the ones that apply to you last minute changes feeling neglected feeling disrespected stress at work unrealistic expectations over commitment hurtful words not being heard yelling feeling controlled manipulation misunderstood.

Main Points to Consider _____

_____

_____

_____

_____

_____

_____

_____

_____

_____

Break Out: Wife

Talk about an issue this week in your husband-wife meeting. Practice conflict resolution.

Below are areas that we are most susceptible to anger.

Discuss the ones that apply to you last minute changes feeling neglected feeling disrespected stress at work unrealistic expectations over commitment hurtful words disobedient children yelling feeling controlled manipulation misunderstood

Main Points to Consider_____

_____

_____

_____

_____

_____

_____

_____

_____

_____

Chapter 3
Forgiveness

In our marriage conferences, we often ask, every couple that has ever considered divorce to stand up. Usually the whole room is standing, unless there is a newlywed couple in the crowd.

That tells us something about the dynamic of marriage. It just isn't as easy as we've seen in the movies. Offences will come in abundance. They are a staple of relationships. While they are often painful and tiresome, they help us to grow and mature. We learn that everything isn't as dramatic as we imagine in the moment. We learn how to weather the storms and develop the fruit of longsuffering.

The only *real* difference between the marriage of 5 years that breaks up and the marriage of 45 years that is thriving is the power to forgive. Couples are often locked in hard and embittered hearts when they reach the divorce court. They have held on to and collected offenses. They have not learned the real power of extending mercy. That 45 year old marriage has seen far more offense than the 5 year marriage that gave up. The 45 year old relationship continued to choose forgiveness along the way.

So forgiveness plays a huge part in a marriage that survives a lifetime. If we think about it, it plays a huge part in all relationships. But somehow we find it easier to offer others mercy over our spouses. We can forgive our siblings, parents, children, etc. But when it comes to our husband or wife, we just don't want to forgive. It has something to do with the vows that we took. See, we never took a vow with other relationships. We were born into them. So your mom is your mom regardless. A child doesn't stop being your child because of the wrong choices he/she makes. But there is a unique dynamic to marriage. God chose the marriage relationship to demonstrate his relationship with the church. We aren't born into it initially. We must make a choice to love Him and to live with Him forever. Then we are born again. And we can break covenant with Him if we so choose. The same way we can make that choice in a marriage. Yet God expects us to keep covenant with Him and our one flesh partner.

Forgiveness is a holy response to an offense. It is the act of releasing the offender even though he or she is guilty. Granting forgiveness is a choice to set your spouse free from the debt of their offense. It is an attitude of letting go of resentment and vengeance. It is the way Christ responded to our sin. He released us even though we were guilty. He didn't require that we pay for the offense. He paid it for us. If we can love like Jesus, we will receive what God intended.

Forgiveness is also the first step toward rebuilding trust. The scripture reminds us that we ought to forgive others if we want God to forgive us. So we must have an abundance of mercy in order for our marriages to thrive. So often we find that people apply mercy to themselves but practice law when it comes to others. We all have sinned and fell short of God's magnificent glory. So there are times when we will all stand in need of mercy. And God has designed it where there will be times when we will need to extend mercy.

If Christ is to be formed in us, certainly we must practice mercy. He allows us the holy opportunity to awaken to a new mercy every morning. And we have been guilty of some damnable things.

So there should be no one that we can't forgive; especially our one flesh partners.

It's interesting that we said that we would love for better or for worse. But what is the worse? It's all the stuff that will be a challenge for us to forgive. If we were to write a list of what we would consider "the worse", it would help us to understand this covenant we have bonded ourselves to. All the hard stuff falls under the category of worse. So we have to grow in forgiveness and that forgiveness cannot be conditional. God grants us unconditional, whole mercy. Even if we think that something is just unpardonable, it isn't. Jesus covered it all with His blood. And He says if we choose to not forgive, we won't be forgiven. We reap the mercy that we sow to others.

If we are truly forgiving, we do not store up offenses for a rainy day. We should not bring up a past offense to strengthen a present argument. This is unfair. It proves that the present defense is not strong enough to stand on its own. When we walk in forgiveness we refuse to rehearse an old offense. Holding a wound over your spouse's head is manipulative and destructive. If we continue to bring it up, it is like pulling a scab off a healing wound. We do more harm to ourselves than good. If we truly forgive, we must leave the past in the past.

"*Forgiveness is the scent that the rose leaves on the heel that crushes it*" - Source unknown.

Forgiveness is a choice, not an emotion. You choose it long before you feel it. Your brain must get the message to your heart. It is not the other way around. You never feel it first. Emotions can be very volatile.

As you make the choice to forgive, you must remember that:

YOUR MATE IS NOT YOUR ENEMY!!! Even if it feels like he/she is. He/She is not! Don't lose sight of this. <u>Your goal is to restore oneness in your relationship.</u> That requires forgiveness.

Brethren, If a man be overtaken in a fault, ye which are spiritual, restore, such an one in the spirit of meekness; considering thyself, lest thy also be tempted. Galatians 6:1

Break Out: Husband

1. Other than Jesus Christ, whom do you look to as an example of a forgiving person? (Explain your answer).
2. What time in your life was significant in you remembering having to say, "I'm sorry?"
3. What time in your life do you remember most that you had to forgive someone else?
4. What person in your life stands out with the ability to hold a grudge?

Read Matthew 6:14-15 and Matthew 18:21-22. Identify what stands out to you in these scriptures.

Main Points to Consider_____

_____

_____

_____

_____

_____

_____

_____

Break Out: Wife

1. Other than Jesus Christ, whom do you look to as an example of a forgiving person? (Explain your answer).
2. What time in your life was significant in you remembering having to say, "I'm sorry?"
3. What time in your life do you remember most that you had to forgive someone else?
4. What person in your life stands out with the ability to hold a grudge?

Read Matthew 6:14-15 and Matthew 18:21-22. Identify what stands out to you in these scriptures

Main Points to Consider_____

_____

_____

_____

_____

_____

_____

_____

_____

Chapter 4
Parenting/Step-parenting

There is no real difference between the approach to step-parenting and parenting. So whether you have children and/or step-children, the method is the same. Your parenting wisdom must come directly from the Word of God. Certainly there are different challenges that arise in step-parenting. However, the basic approach to parenting is the same.

First of all, we need to understand that parenting is a team effort. It involves both parents (and sets of parents), and most importantly the Lord. The team approach minimizes the chances of manipulation by the children. The old African proverb says that it takes a village to raise a child. It is important to not only have the village in place, but that the village is on one accord.

Conflict can arise if parents do not have a relationship with the Lord. But even if only one parent has a relationship with God, the parenting can be successful. Ask God's blessing not just on your children, but on the step-parents and all those involved in the decision-making for the child.

A basic premise of parenting is never let the children divide you. Even if you disagree, present a united front in the presence of the children. Discuss later (when alone) the areas of disagreement. Then come back together to make adjustments (if necessary). But you should never ever argue in front of them. It makes children uncomfortable and will sometimes force them to choose sides.

At other times, it is an opportunity for a child to use it to

his/her best interest (manipulation).
Support each other in the discipline that is meted out. Do not override each other. It undermines the authority of the disciplining parent.

Be consistent in discipline. If you say it, abide by it. If you are constantly changing your mind or not enforcing discipline, children will be unsure of their boundaries. If that happens, they will push the limits. Because they know you don't really mean what your say. Offer your children loving correction. The Bible says that you hate your children if you do not chastise them. Be consistent. But be just. Make sure the punishment fits the offense. Don't go over the top for a simple infraction.

Family meetings should be instituted for effective communication. We are firm believers that children should be heard. Family meetings allow a child the opportunity to voice his opinion (respectfully) even if he/she disagrees with a rule or discipline. Talk to your children. When they become teenagers, this will take more effort. But find out what is going on in their lives. Pray for *and* with your children. And certainly, model the behavior you want them to emulate.

Seize teachable moments, they will present themselves regularly. Build godly character through instruction, discipline and modeling the proper example. Recognize each child is an individual, not part of the group. Get to know each one separately. Help them discover their unique purpose and pursue their dreams. Establish family time once a week. Build memories.

Plan activities together as a family:

Rent a movie
Go to the playground
Play a board game or video game
Go to the kids' favorite restaurant
Bake cookies together

The activity is not what's most important; but the time spent together enjoying one another. So if a child wants to repeat an activity by all means, allow it.

There is no such thing as the perfect parent. Both of your parents have made mistakes in raising you. And you, too, will make mistakes in your approach to parenting. We guarantee that your children **WILL** have their own complaints. Nevertheless, parent with confidence. Trust your instincts. Bathe your decision making in prayer and the Word.

Give your children the best of you. Don't try to be their friends. They will have an opportunity to have a host of friends. They only have the opportunity to have you as their parents. So parent well. Love them lavishly.

Give them your time and your energy. Be there for them. Give loads of affection and affirmation. Attend their events. Cheer them on. Make pleasant memories.

Husbands, emulate the type of man you want your daughter to marry. Treat your wife in such a way that your daughter desires that for herself and your son learns how to treat a woman. Wives, be the woman that you want your sons to choose and daughters to imitate because most certainly they will learn from what they see.

Here are the **Do Nots**:

* Do not yell and scream at your children

* Do not call your children out of their names

* Do not spank children when you are emotionally out of control. (Whichever parent is least emotional, this one needs to administer the discipline).

* Do not spank a child for every infraction or it becomes ineffective. (Try other forms of discipline before spanking). *Do not spank a teenager (agree upon a cut-off for spankings usually around age 11 or 12)

* Do not give a discipline that you have no intention of following through on.

* Do not treat your children all the same. They have different needs and personalities.

* Do not favor one child over another.

* Do not provoke your children to anger.

* Do not spoil your child(ren).

Break Out: Husband

1. Think of a time when you thought you were disciplined unfairly. What happened?
2. Think of a time when you could have used more parental oversight? What might have been the result?
3. Look at parents around you (other than your own). Which parents do you most admire and why?
4. What is something that your parents did that you especially enjoyed?

The purpose of the assignment was to help you to see things you may incorporate or may not want to incorporate as a parent. What are some things you would like to do differently than your own parents?

Main Points to Consider_____

_____

_____

_____

_____

_____

_____

_____

Break Out: Wife

1. Think of a time when you thought you were disciplined unfairly. What happened?
2. Think of a time when you could have used more parental oversight? What might have been the result?
3. Look at parents around you (other than your own). Which parents do you most admire? Why?
4. What is something that your parents did that you especially enjoyed?

The purpose of the assignment was to help you to see things you may incorporate or may not want to incorporate as a parent. What are some things you would like to do differently than your own parents?

Main Points to Consider _____

_____

_____

_____

_____

_____

_____

_____

Chapter 5
Oneness

In order for a couple to experience true intimacy, they must set aside their own selfishness and follow God's plan for marriage. The heart of a Oneness Marriage is an intensely spiritual relationship. God *must* be central!

#1 Believe your spouse is a gift from God. Marriage is His design and idea. So accept your gift, be grateful for your gift. And honor the Giver of such an amazing gift. Your gift will have complications and challenges. Yet he/she is perfect for you. This may seem easy to believe right now. But later on you may be challenged in seeing your spouse this way. But always go back to this foundational thought - Why did I get married? And understand that you got married because it was God's idea for humankind. And He wanted to bless you with a special gift of this husband/wife.

#2 Leave all others. In order to become one with this special person, all others must become secondary in your relationship. This includes parents, siblings, and friends. You both have new best friends - each other. So work to build that relationship. You become each other's main source of emotional, spiritual, and physical support, (after the Lord of course). Families and individual spouses sometimes find this breaking away painful. It doesn't have to be that way if handled with wisdom. Include your family in your life. "Leaving" your loved ones does not mean you should have nothing to do with them. It means adjusting them in the area of priority. They no longer hold first place in your heart or life. There is an intimate area of your marriage that only belongs to each other.

#3 Cleave to your mate. You must be loyal and committed

to your spouse. People often secretly think if this marriage doesn't work out, I can try again with someone else. This is self-defeating. It's like leaving a large hole in your marriage. And it is destined for failure. You seal it when you make a firm and full commitment. Your commitment should be unconditional and irrevocable. Marriage was meant to last a lifetime. God commands us that we must keep covenant. If we approach the relationship like it is forever, than we will work to make it last.

#4 <u>Receive</u> the process of becoming one flesh. Work on oneness in all areas after you are married. Becoming one involves uniting the entirety of 2 individuals. Embrace the full process with enthusiasm. You will become one in 5 primary areas:

A) Spiritually, as you seek the Lord, together.

B) Financially, as you share your belongings and wealth together.

C) Intimately by sharing your hearts and dreams.

D) Physically by handling life's difficulties together.

E) Sexually by uniting your bodies together.

Break Out: Husband

1. Do you see your wife as a gift from God? Explain your answer.

2. Can you think of any areas that your families will find it difficult to let you leave?

3. How will you handle that?

4. What areas do you think will be more of a challenge at becoming one?

5. Have you shared things that have happened in your marriage with others outside of the relationship? (friends and family)

6. If so, how has that affected your relationship?

Main Points to Consider _____

_____

_____

_____

_____

_____

_____

_____

_____

Breakout: Wife

1. Do you see your husband as a gift from God? Explain your answer.
2. Can you think of any areas that your families will find it difficult to let you leave?
3. How will you handle that?
4. What areas do you think will be more of a challenge at becoming one?
5. Have you shared things that have happened in your marriage with others outside of the relationship?
6. If so, how has that affected your relationship?

Main Points to Consider _____

_____

_____

_____

_____

_____

_____

_____

_____

Chapter 6
In-laws

The term "in-laws" has a negative connotation in our culture. You have heard the numerous "in-law" jokes. However in-laws are only negative when they bring unwanted interference into the marriage relationship. The in-law relationship does not have to be negative.

There are a number of families who have amazing in-law relationships. The Bible says that Ruth was better to her mother-in-law than 7 sons. What a beautiful testimony! Jethro gave sound advice to Moses, his son-in-law. Moses took heed and was blessed. So the in-law relationship can be a wonderful blessing. It all depends on our perspective.

Many times in-laws have good intentions. But they go about applying those intents in the wrong way. Most have never heard any teaching on the in-law relation. And simply do not understand their role.

The word "in-law" simply means that you gain a new parent or sibling by law. The marriage ceremony ties the two families together. Newlyweds should look to join families instead of entering the relationship with a more divisive outlook. Certainly a man must leave his parents and cleave to his spouse but it does not mean that you abort the families. Had Ruth's husband aborted his relationship with his parents, Naomi and Ruth would not have had the blessing of their relationship. Sometimes, we find that the new spouse will cling to his/her own family and doesn't allow room for the new family. This makes it difficult for the in-laws to clearly define their role. They often feel excluded or a sense of loss. The responsibility will fall on the married couple to help their parents and siblings balance their love, and be inclusive in relating.

Make room in your heart and live for your new family. Somehow, all are touched by the in-law relationship. Most daughters-in-law will someday become a mother-in-law, and so forth. Because of that, spouses should become more empathetic to make the relationship work. Sow the relationship you want to reap. If you want your mother-in-law to treat you like a daughter then make sure you are treating her like a mom. The scriptures remind us to do unto others as we would have others do unto us (St. Matthew 7:12)

The problems that arise in the in-law relationship usually are a result of either meddling relatives, relatives who do not like each other, or those who do not know each other well enough. So as a married couple, how do you handle the delicate in-law relationship?

#1 First of all, remember to be loyal to your spouse. Being loyal means covering your spouse when you are relating with your family. It is okay to seek godly wisdom from your parents. Parents can be a great help to a new marriage. But spouses must always seek to *protect the spouse when soliciting wisdom.* Don't run to your family with every little issue. Try to work it out on your own first. And don't tear down your spouse to your family. Often a spouse will share every negative trait about their spouse and make themselves out to be the innocent bystander. When in fact there is much more to the story than has been shared. It doesn't matter how serious the offense, the spouse must be sensitive when sharing information about the marriage.

When you two have been restored and have forgiven one another, family members still remember the offense. If you paint your spouse in an unfavorable light, it can cause permanent damage to the in-law relationship. Protect your spouse always. Be respectful and just. When possible, couples should seek advice together, so parents get a balanced view. Never slander your spouse to your parents and/or siblings. Even if your spouse is acting unseemly, you must be very careful how you talk about it to your family. It is unproductive to the marriage to get them to side with you. If you are ever in this position, it is best to get advice outside of the family circle.

#2 Know your parents' strength and weaknesses. Know what they can and cannot handle before seeking advice. Agree with your spouse what you will and will not discuss with them. If your parents are not strong communicators, you don't want to take a communication issue to them. If a subject matter could cause an argument to occur in their relationship, be sensitive enough not to bring it up. Couples have to be prudent in how they access that information base. In order for their knowledge to be effective in your lives, you need to be selective in what you ask.

#3 Just because your parents give advice, doesn't mean you are obligated to act on it. If the advice is not in the best interest of the relationship, it should not be followed. *All counsel should be godly.* The counsel should consider both parties. And never should the counsel favor one over the other. In most cases, parents will side with their offspring. Not all parents do, but most will.

If you know that your parents or siblings do not like your spouse, then you *must never* seek marriage advice from them.

You should also buffet any of their attempts to exclude your spouse or damage your relationship. If they invite you to family events and do not welcome your spouse, you should not accept. You must be adamant about his/her inclusion. Demand that he/she be respected as your one flesh partner. These are immature attempts to divide you from your spouse. Let your family know how you feel about your spouse's exclusion. Some families are so bad that they won't call the house because the in-law might answer; thus they only contact the family member by cell phone. In this case, families should not be offered access to the one party. It is critical to the relationship that they be directed to call the home number. Of course, if you can't make this work, find another avenue. The most important thing to remember is to **NEVER** allow anyone else to set the tone for your relationship.

Once you say, "I Do", you begin the process of becoming one. Let no one divide you. This important principle of marriage is found in Genesis 2:24, Therefore shall a man **leave** his father and his mother, and shall ***cleave*** unto his wife: and they shall be one flesh. God clearly wanted us to understand this. Because when Adam spoke this, he didn't have a mother and father to leave. It is a word of wisdom spoken at the very beginning, when God presented the first marriage.

#4 If there is a conflict between your spouse and your parent, you must be the one who runs interference. You must confront. Your spouse should not be left in the vulnerable and compromising position of having to confront an in-law. A parent or sibling is able to handle conflict from their own child or sibling better than from the in-law (especially in the early years). So be wise and always precede with prayer.

#5 Be reluctant in borrowing money from family members. Money gives unspoken authority. Family members gain illegitimate entry into your personal business. Parents and other family members will give unsolicited advice if they have lent money. They will think they have a right. Often those loans come with many invisible strings and cost more than what you originally bargained. So proceed with caution.

#6 It is not Christ-like to render evil for evil. We are to overcome evil with good. We don't dislike someone, because they dislike us. We must do everything in our power to make relationships work. The Bible says that we must follow peace with all men, as much as it lies within our power. Every attempt should be made to make the in-law relationships work.

One of the most important things you can do is sow time, honor, and respect into your in-law relationship. This is your spouse's family which he/she loves. Even if your husband/wife seems nonchalant about his/her family, you should always regard those family members with respect. It is honoring to a spouse when the other makes a conscious effort to esteem the in-laws. Spend time developing your relationship with your in-laws. This is your new family. It is true that when you marry the spouse, you marry the family. Sow good works into your parents-in-law. Do not wait until they start acting "right". You must take the first step. And by all means, do not criticize your in-laws in front of your children.

The Bible admonishes us to love the unlovable; to pray for, and do good to those who hate us and despitefully use us. Pray over your relationship; even if starts out rocky, God has the ability to turn it around.

Breakout: Husband

On a scale of 1 to 10, with 10 being the best…

1. Rate your relationship with your father.

    1 2 3 4 5 6 7 8 9 10

2. Rate your relationship with your mother.
    1 2 3 4 5 6 7 8 9 10

3. Do you spend time or talk to your parents on a regular basis (at least monthly)?
    Yes   No

4. If not, why?

5. How do you feel about your parent's marriage(s)?

6. What are areas of concern with your parents?

Main Points to Consider

_____

_____

_____

_____

_____

_____

Breakout: Wife

On a scale of 1 to 10 with 10 being the best.

1. Rate your relationship with your father.
    1 2 3 4 5 6 7 8 9 10

2. Rate your relationship with your mother.
    1 2 3 4 5 6 7 8 9 10

3. Do you spend time or talk to your parents on a regular basis (at least monthly)?
    Yes   No

4. If not, why?

5. How do you feel about your parent's marriage(s)?

6. What are areas of concern with your parents?

Main Points to Consider _____

_____

_____

_____

_____

_____

_____

Parent Project: Husband

Set aside a time when you can call your parents and your in-laws to work through the following questionnaire over the phone or in person. It is best done in person. Be sure to set aside sufficient time to go over these questions and give them ample time to think about their answers. You may want to give them the questions ahead of time, so they can think about and discuss their answers.

Ask your parents, the following questions:

1. What does the ideal marriage look like to you?

_____

_____

2. What was the biggest challenge in your marriage? Why?

_____

_____

3. If you could keep one memory or experience in all your married life, what would it be and why?

_____

_____

4. If you could start all over, what would you do differently in your marriage?

_____

_____

5. Do you feel included in our lives? If no,
   Why?

_____

_____

6. How do you think my relationship with you, could   change for the better, considering that I am married and establishing my own family and home?

_____

_____

7. Do you feel we have handled holidays properly?

YES   NO   SOMEWHAT

8. Do you feel involved in the lives of our children? Or how would you like to be involved when we begin to have children?

_____

_____

_____

9. Can you give me advice to balance work, husband, children, church responsibilities, and other commitments?

_____

_____

_____

_____

_____

_____

_____

_____

_____

_____

_____

_____

Parent Project:
Husband (continued)

Ask your in-laws these questions:

1. How was your relationship with your in-laws?

_____

_____

2. Is there any wisdom that you can offer me about your daughter to help me be the husband that she needs?

_____

_____

3. How would you describe my relationship with you?

a) Not, the best
b) Okay, but room for improvement
c) Great, keep it up!

4. What advice can you give me to better our relationship?

_____

_____

6. What changes can you make to better our relationship?

_____

_____

7. I call you _____, is that okay with you?

8. What would you like your future grandchildren to call you?

_____

Parent Project: Wife

Set aside a time when you can call your parents and your in-laws to go through the questionnaire over the phone or in person. It is best done in person. Be sure to set aside sufficient time to go over these questions and give them ample time to think about their answers. You may want to give them the questions ahead of time, so they can think about and discuss their answers.

Ask your parents, the following questions:

1. What does the ideal marriage look like to you?

_____

_____

2. What was the biggest challenge in your marriage? Why?

_____

_____

3. If you could keep one memory or experience in all your married life, what would it be and why?

_____

_____

4. If you could start all over, what would you do differently in your marriage?

_____

_____

5. Do you feel included in our lives? If no, Why?

_____

_____

6. How do you think my relationship with you, could change for the better, considering that I am married and establishing my own family and home?

_____

_____

7. Do you feel we have handled holidays properly?

YES   NO   SOMEWHAT

8. Do you feel involved in the lives of our children? Or how would you like to be involved when we begin to have children?

_____

_____

9. Can you give me advice to balance work, husband, children, church responsibilities, and other commitments?

_____

_____

_____

_____

_____

_____

_____

_____

_____

_____

_____

_____

_____

Parent Project:
Wife (continued)

Ask your in-laws these questions:

1. How was your relationship with your in-laws?

_____

_____

2. Is there any wisdom that you can offer me about your son to help me be the wife that he needs?

_____

_____

3. How would you describe my relationship with you?

a) Not, the best
b) Okay, but room for improvement
c) Great, keep it up!

4. What advice can you give me to better our relationship?

_____

_____

_____

5. What changes can you make to better our relationship?

_____

_____

6. I call you _____, is that okay with you?

7. What would you like your future grandchildren to call you?_____

Chapter 7
Power Struggles

Power struggles occur when either husband or wife reach a stalemate in the relationship. It is usually the result of one or both being selfish; and demanding that things be done their own way. It is married persons locked in a battle of wills.

In order for a marriage to be successful, there must be a sufficient amount of give and take in the relationship. A husband should not demand to be the head. And the wife should not insist on having her own way. This will cause contention and strife. Ephesians 5:21 tells us to submit ourselves one to another in the fear of God.

Marriage is about serving one another. If we see the picture of Jesus as bridegroom in relationship with His bride, we understand the marriage dynamic, which the scripture says, is a great mystery. Christ, as the head, lovingly serves His bride. But the Bride is also called upon to serve Him as King. It is a two-sided relationship.

Successful couples will work to come to an agreement. It is always best if the two are on one accord. Both parties should discuss his/her position on a matter. These issues should be respectfully considered in a non-threatening and open environment. Spouses should be sympathetic to each other. It is not helpful to attack the other because you don't agree.

We know that a house divided against itself cannot stand. Oneness is the strength to any marriage. But that marriage will unravel when spouses become single-minded and independent. Operate as a vital part of a team.

Power struggles cannot germinate in an environment where there is a team mindset. Couples must make decisions based upon what is in the best interest of their team. That team includes husband, wife and children. Neither spouse should seek his or her own way.

 The wisdom of Proverbs says, one will put a thousand to flight and two, ten thousand. If couples align their power together over the enemy, they are able to triumph over him. The power of agreement defeats the enemy in your relationship.

When couples are in the midst of conflict, the best thing to do is to separate the emotion from the actual issue. The emotion is what keeps the power struggle in tact. If we learn how to separate our issues and concerns from the emotions, we will defeat our adversary every time. In the midst of a squabble, you need to ask yourself, what is most important? Hopefully, you will answer this question correctly with "my relationship". The wrong answers are "getting my way" or "being right".

The fleshly tendency is to withdraw from your spouse in the heat of an argument. However we are to walk in the Spirit. We, as believers, do not walk in the flesh. So, choose the opposite of the flesh. Touch, in the midst of the argument. Embrace, hold hands, and squeeze his /her shoulder. Connect physically in some way. This helps to remove the emotion from the issue.

 Power struggles are a lot like civil wars. They can do more damage to a relationship than any outside enemy. Too often, husband thinks his way is right, and wife thinks her way is best. However, it may be that you both are wrong or you both are right. Spend time in prayer asking God for his wisdom. Let His peace and grace under gird your relationship. Surrender to the King of kings.

Trust Him to lead your relationship.

If a couple reaches an impasse, the scripture clearly says that Christ is the head of every man. And the man is the head of his wife (I Corinthians 11:3). God is a God of order. A wife is to acquiesce in matters of the marriage and home to the leading of her husband. Her submission to God hinges on her submission to her husband. She should not override his leadership.

Likewise, ye wives, be in subjection to your own husbands; that, if any obey not the word, they also may without the word be won by the conversation of the wives. I Peter 3:1

Wives submit yourselves unto your own husbands, as unto the Lord. Ephesians 5:22

For the husband is the head of the wife even as Christ is the head of the church: and he is the savior of the body. Eph 5:23

Therefore as the church is subject unto Christ, so let the wives be to their own husbands in every thing. Ephesians 5:24

Even so it is the wise husband that listens to his wife and considers what she has to say.

(For more help, revisit the chapter 2 on Communication and Conflict Resolution)

.

Break Out: Husband

1. Pick an instance where you had an issue.
2. How could you have handled it differently in light of this assignment?
3. Give an instance where you saw a couple engaged in a power struggle.
4. What happened?
5. What did you think about it?

Read Ephesians 5:22-33. Which particular scripture(s) stood out to you?

Main Points to Consider _____

_____

_____

_____

_____

_____

_____

_____

_____

_____

Break Out: Wife

1. Pick an instance where you had an issue.
2. How could you have handled it differently in light of this assignment?
3. Give an instance where you saw a couple engaged in a power struggle.
4. What happened?
5. What did you think about it?

Read Ephesians 5:22-33. Which particular scripture(s) stood out to you?

_____

_____

_____

_____

_____

_____

_____

_____

_____

Chapter 8
Unrealistic Expectations

Unrealistic Expectations can destroy a marriage. Often times, couples have ideas about how the marriage will proceed and these ideas are in direct opposition to reality. They want marriage to fulfill all their desires. Couples are often ignorant to the truth of marriage. Most are looking for something magical to happen in marriage. And when it doesn't, there is a lot of disappointment.

Women are looking for a knight in shining armor to rescue them from their problems and their lives. They look forward to eating out, going on picnics and having fresh flowers delivered to their jobs; including a host of other romantic gestures.

 Some fantasize that they will never argue. She will spend her days shopping and spending. She won't have any money concerns, once she is married. She and hubby will have a big house and nice things. They will go to movies, and plays, and concerts. Yes, life will be quite good.

Men, on the other hand, are looking for a Princess Maid. She will come in and cook, clean, wash, iron, work a job and then give him all the sex he wants, whenever he wants and in the midst of it all, she will keep herself looking good for him and raise their many children.

Not only that, while she is busy raising his children and cleaning his house, he gets to sit back and put his feet up and watch whatever he wants on television; after she draws his bath and gives him a massage.

Neither of these are realistic pictures of a successful marriage. Another side of unrealistic expectations is the Pollyanna perspective. Christian couples are particularly susceptible to this thinking:

- My mate is able to meet all my needs.
- Feelings of love and passion will never fade.
- Life will always be fun and exciting
- Now that we are married, I won't be lonely.
- I will be able to help my mate become a better person.
- Our marriage will be without issues because we are Christians

Too many couples enter marriage blinded by unreasonable expectations. The reality is that *your mate is not going to meet every one of your needs.* He/she is not equipped to meet all of your expectations. Christ alone holds that position. If your spouse was able to do that, what would you need with a Savior? He/She is a human being with faults. There is no way possible for your mate to meet all of your needs.

Your feelings of excitement will fade. Feelings are not reliable. You made a commitment to love. Hold on to that regardless of the feelings. You will have peaks and valleys in your relationship. Love is a choice not an emotion.

You may have periods of loneliness in the marriage. They are thousands of lonely spouses on the earth. Disappointments come in what we find and what we expect to find don't match. So it is very possible to be in a relationship and feel loneliness. God is able to help you through those tough seasons.

You will have disagreements and arguments even though you are Christians. When you were single, you had trouble with your own flesh. Now you add to that dynamic, another human with flesh. It's called double trouble. The assignment to become one in Spirit for two individuals with living flesh is complicated. Sometimes that flesh will clash.

You will not be able to change your mate. You can barely change things that you don't like within yourself. So how in the world will you be able to change another person? You can't. Jesus is the only one who can change the hearts of men. So give up on trying to make your spouse better. Work on making a better you.

Each of us **brings** a certain set of expectations, a mental picture of how we will live, behave, and interact in the marriage. The challenge for most couples is to identify the expectations that may lead to conflict later in the relationship and take a more realistic approach.

Break Out: Husband

What do you think of each of the following statements?

1. We had counseling therefore we won't have as many problems as others.
2. Our children will be brilliant and much better-behaved than other children.
3. We won't argue because we understand one another.
4. We won't have any financial struggles because we know how to do a budget.
5. Our parents had strong marriages, so we will too.

Discuss these and any other unrealistic expectations
that the two of you may have.

_____

_____

_____

_____

_____

_____

_____

_____

Break Out: Wife

<u>What do you think of each of the following statements?</u>

1. We had counseling therefore we won't have as many problems as others.
2. Our children will be brilliant and much better-behaved than other children.
3. We won't argue because we understand one another.
4. We won't have any financial struggles because we know how to do a budget.
5. Our parents had strong marriages, so we will too.

Discuss these and any other unrealistic expectations that the two of you may have.

_____

_____

_____

_____

_____

_____

_____

_____

Chapter 9
Money Matters

The earth is the Lord's and all it contains, the world, and those who dwell in it. Psalm 24:1

Money in lack or abundance has divided many couples. This is still one of the top reasons couples divorce. You do not have to allow issues concerning money to divide you. You both should have a working knowledge of your budget and debts (even if only one is working). But one of you should be primarily responsible for overseeing your spending and savings plans. Determine which of you has the financial management strength. This person should coordinate the spending plan. But both husband and wife should be involved in *all* financial decisions. There have been countless stories of partners who died and the spouse didn't have a clue as to the state of their finances. So be involved by all means.

Listed are ways to prevent financial tension:

■ Avoid money secrets: Hidden purchases, concealed debts (credit cards, traffic tickets, etc.), confidential bonuses or pay increases, secret bank accounts, lending money to a relative behind your spouses back; or one or both spouses not sticking to an agreed upon spending plan. These covert financial operations can cost you a healthy relationship.

It is important that you operate as one in your finances - working from one (money) pot. Everything that comes in, goes to the one pot. Separate bank accounts can be very divisive and create a myriad of troubles.

You can have as many accounts as you choose, but both spouses should have access to all accounts.

That requires being open and honest about your spending and income. Financial oneness requires trust. If a breach has occurred in the relationship, work on rebuilding it. In order to have a successful marriage you must trust one another.

Financial oneness requires that you do what is in the best interest of your immediate family. This does not include extended family, because those interests can conflict. Agree ahead of time to whom you will lend money and what is the maximum amount to any one person. This may change as you enter different financial seasons. So be sure to revisit it from time to time. Agree that *nothing* will be hid from the other, except special surprises for the spouse. And under no circumstances should you ever co-sign for anyone. If for some reason that person no longer has the ability to pay, that debt becomes yours. The scriptures warn us about co-signing. *He that is surety for a stranger shall smart for it: and he that hateth suretyship is sure. Proverbs 12:15*

- Keep first things first. If couples have different priorities they will not be able to operate on one accord. Example: Wife was off work for a week because of illness. Her pay was cut. So there is now less income to pay the bills. Wife wants to pay her hospital bill. Husband wants to pay the gas bill. Or couple has a large tax refund, husband wants to put down payment on a new house, wife wants to save it.

  Prayer is the best offense to handling sticky issues like this one. Seek wisdom from the heart of God.

- Addictions are also a financial pit. Whether it be drug

addiction, porn addiction, coffee addiction, or even an addiction to a hobby (golf, bowling, video games, etc.) It can take a financial toll on the family. At the root of all addictions are selfishness and pride. The goal is all about satisfying flesh. Addictions are best, broken. Seek the Lord for deliverance. Do not feed addictions, these monsters will destroy your family.

- <u>Lack of Preparation is also a trouble spot</u>. When couples do not save for rainy days or unexpected expenses, it eats into their general fund and causes them to fall short. Most material possessions will not last forever. Car repairs and maintenance, appliance repairs, medical expenses are certain. They will absolutely, positively be needed. So plan for them. Put something away every pay period to cover those needs.

Also some couples experience seasonal boons and droughts in their income based upon their professions. Know when those times are and prepare for them. Tax preparers work from December to April. Teachers sometimes are not paid through the summer. Some contractors are seasonal. Prepare for those seasons of lesser income.

Planning for the future is also pertinent. You must plan for retirement, children's college funds, etc. Make sure you have a will and each of you is the beneficiary on insurance policies. If a couple has prepared financially, they can avert many financial disasters.

- <u>Lack of knowledge is another danger in dealing with money issues</u>. If only one spouse knows the state of the finances, the other tends to overspend because he/she is unaware as to the state of their flocks (so to speak). In

73

becoming one, both parties need to be fully informed; knowing passwords, what hasn't been paid, what has been paid, what is in savings, how much insurance, etc. (There are exceptions to this rule - drug or alcohol addiction).

The most important thing you can do is to communicate about money. Have a regular time where you sit down together and go over the finances once or twice a month. Talk about issues before they arise and how you will handle them (aging parents, or if one spouse loses his/her job).

It is also helpful in the untimely death of one of the spouses to know where you stand financially. The surviving spouse will need to be fully aware of what money is available and what debts are at hand.

Breakout: Husband

1. Are you a saver or a spender?
2. Did you grow up in poverty?
3. How important is good credit to you?
4. Do your parents have good credit?
5. Did your parents spend a lot of money on you as a child?
6. Will you spend a lot of money on your child(ren)?
7. Do you pay bills on time?

Main Points to Consider _____

_____

_____

_____

_____

_____

_____

_____

_____

_____

_____

Breakout: Wife

1. Are you a saver or a spender?
2. Did you grow up in poverty?
3. How important is good credit to you?
4. Do your parents have good credit?
5. Did your parents spend a lot of money on you as a child?
6. Will you spend a lot of money on your child(ren)?
7. Do you pay bills on time?

Main Points to Consider _____

_____

_____

_____

_____

_____

_____

_____

_____

_____

Break Out: Husband & Wife

1. How much total debt do we have?

    $ _____

2.What will we do to get out of debt?

_____

_____

3. Do we operate on a budget?   YES   NO

4. Will we borrow?   YES   NO

5. Will we lend?   YES   NO

6. What does it mean *the borrower is a servant to the lender*?

_____

_____

7. Will we cosign for family members and friends?
YES   NO   MAYBE

8. Who will handle the money, pay the bills, etc.?
Wife   Husband

9. What will our approach be to savings, investments, insurance, etc.?

_____

_____

10.How will we prepare, if we are forced to go to one income?

_____

_____

11. Will we tithe and give offerings?   YES   NO

12. How will we make money decisions?

A) On the spot
B) after 24 hours
C) wait a week
D) after prayer and going over budget plan

13. Cosigning: what if your parents split up and one of them comes to you for help? They need you to cosign to help them out just until they can get on their feet. What will you say?

_____

_____

14. Who does the money belong to?

a) Hers
b) His
c) Ours
d) God's

Chapter 10
Sexual Intimacy

God designed sex to be a vital fiery expression of love in marriage.

Therefore shall a man leave his father and mother and shall cleave unto his wife: and they shall be one flesh. And they were both naked the man and his wife and were not ashamed. Gen 2:24-25

Sex is a beautiful act to God in the context of marriage.
He intended for both partners to receive mutual enjoyment.
When we read Song of Solomon, we see the experience shared through prose.

Let him kiss me with the kisses of his mouth: for thy love is better than wine. Song 1:2

Some have interpreted it to be a literal love affair between a king and his bride. Some describe it as God's relationship to Israel. Others count it as a word of prophecy regarding Christ and the church. Song of Solomon is all of that. God's word is multi-faceted. Let's look at the passages in Chapter 7:1-10. See how he describes his bride's body:

How beautiful are thy feet with shoes; O prince's daughter! The joints of thy thighs are like jewels, the work of the hands of a cunning workman.

Thy navel is like a round goblet, which wanteth not liquor: thy belly is like an heap of wheat set about with lilies.

Thy two breasts are like two young roes that are twins.

Thy neck is as a tower of ivory; thine eyes like the fishpools in Hesh'-bon, by the gate of Bathrabbim: thy nose is as the tower of Lebanon which looketh toward Damascus.

Thine head upon thee is like Carmel, and the hair of thine head like purple; the king is held in the galleries. How fair and how pleasant art thou, O love, for delights!

This thy stature is like to a palm tree, and thy breasts to clusters of grapes. I said, I will go up to the palm tree, I will take hold of the boughs thereof: now also thy breasts shall be as clusters of the vine, and the smell of thy nose like apples;

And the roof of thy mouth like the best wine for my beloved, that goeth down sweetly, causing the lips of those that are asleep to speak. I am my beloved's, and his desire is toward me.

What a beautiful description! God wants us to understand something here. The bride's body is to be a delight to her bridegroom and vice-versa (chapter 5).

We often advise couples to pray together before engaging in the sexual act. God wants to be involved in every aspect of our lives. He is not timid about your sexual relationship. As we can see in the passages above. So take time to ask God's blessing on your sexual union. His word tells us to acknowledge Him in all of our ways, and he will direct our path. God is able to connect the two of you in a way that you've never experienced.

Take time to invite Him in your bedroom. You should also spend time talking about sex. Many married couples never discuss sex, outside of the bedroom, as if its taboo. You are married. Talk about it. Engage in conversations at non-sexual times about what you both prefer. Talk sexy to each other. Leave messages for each other. This will certainly boost your time of intimacy.

If you are not ready to have a baby, make sure that you agree upon the type of birth control that you will implement. Talk to your doctor, about the choices available to you.

To Husbands:

More effort is required to excite a woman sexually; because she is stimulated by the emotional and relational. Therefore a husband should be sensitive to her and seek to ignite her through her emotions. Learn to make love to your wife's heart first and her body will respond. Listen to her, honor her, and serve her. Be there for her, not just physically. Make sure that you are sharing in the household duties as an act of love. This will also insure that she is not overly tired. Pamper her. Leave love notes and messages. Appreciate her. Your sexual experience begins well before you get to the bedroom.

It is appropriate, if you have small children, to put a lock on your door. It's worth the extra $20 or so to make sure that your spouse is comfortable and not worried about a child interrupting.

Take a bath and brush your teeth. Put on cologne. Smells can often change a mood.

Get completely naked (that includes taking off the socks). Touch her body. Explore it. Kiss her. Don't just rush in. Solomon took his time describing each part of his bride's body. Slow it down, gentlemen. You need to be in no hurry. Your wife needs the foreplay. Tell her how wonderful her body is. Massage every part of her body that excites you.

Appreciate her for opening herself up to you physically. Say thank you. Don't take her physical love for granted.

Let her be as the loving hind and pleasant roe; let her breasts satisfy thee at all times; and be thou ravished always with her love. Proverbs 5:19

To Wives:

Men are visual and are turned on by the very sight of the wife's body. It would be in a wife's best interest to arouse her husband visually. Don't turn the lights off every time. Let your husband see your body. Wear sexy lingerie.

Set the atmosphere for your husband. Create an environment in your bedroom that awakes the senses. It should be clean and neat. Use linen spray. Bring in massage oils. Light fragrant candles. Play soft music. Understand that your husband needs to be desired. So initiate sex, sometimes.

He also needs to be affirmed during the love making process. His self image is tied to the sexual experience. So praise him. Your words are key. Do not tell him what he is doing wrong. Gently guide him, if he is going in the wrong direction. Discuss at a later (nonsexual) time, things you like and do not like.

The best way to pleasure your spouse is to approach sex with the mindset of what brings you pleasure. Do not make it your spouse's responsibility to figure out what you want. Go for what you want. It eliminates pressure and stress. And it leaves you both free to enjoy the experience.

Be appreciative of what you have. The quality of your sexual relationship will improve with time. But be grateful for what you have now. Thank your husband for making love to you.

~~

Sometimes couples struggle in their sexual relationship. Many struggles are a direct result of having engaged in premarital sex. Fornication brings many issues to the marriage relationship:

- Comparing spouse to a former lover
- Complications from sexually transmitted diseases
- Fear
- Frigidity
- Health issues
- Impotence
- Inability to have orgasms
- Insecurity
- Premature ejaculation
- Sexual images
- Shame
- Unfulfillment

Couples should understand that these challenges aren't a life sentence. God is a forgiving God and He is able to revive your sexual relationship. Both parties must be honest and open in sharing their struggles. They also must be willing to pray and talk through the issues. The process will require repentance, patience and sensitivity. Sometimes, it may be necessary to contact a health professional or marriage counselor. Be vigilant about protecting your relationship. Don't let pride get in the way of help.

God's Word tells us, *"The wife hath not power of her own body, but the husband: and likewise also the husband hath not power of his own body, but the wife.*

Defraud ye not one the other, except it be with consent for a time, that ye may give yourselves to fasting and prayer; and come together again, that Satan tempt you not for you incontinency"
(I Corinthians 7:4-5)

Husbands and wives should not be in the habit of denying one another. It is important that you come together physically on a regular basis. This pleases God. Couples can get busy and bogged down with the routines of life. This can result in a neglected sex life. Everything does not have to be picture perfect for you to come together. We talked earlier about setting the atmosphere for intimacy. However there will be times when there will be no atmosphere set. No candles. No special scents. No music.

There will be those times when its just the two of you becoming one, physically. So as Nike says, "Just do it". Sex is an important part of the marriage relationship. Don't take it for granted. Sex ties your soul to your spouse, establishing your covenant. So by all means be intimate with one another; with atmosphere and without it.

God Forbid

Sex is a holy act and should not be used as an evil tool of manipulation and control. It is wrong for a wife or husband to decide that she/he will not be intimate with a spouse because some task was not completed as requested. Nor should a spouse deny the other because he/she is not "acting" right. Sex is not to be used as a weapon against a spouse. God is not glorified when we use something that is holy for unholy purposes.

At the same time, spouses should not **demand** sex from one another. Even though Paul gives us a principle in keeping the marriage bed, holy; he also says this is not a command (I Corinthians 7:6). There are times when a wife is unable to pleasure her husband. And her husband needs to be understanding about this. Such times include when she is ill, tired, menstruating, has given birth, following surgery, etc. The couple should work together to make their sexual relationship flow.

In those times, when you can't engage in intercourse, you can still be sexual with one another. Touching, fondling, coddling, kissing are all ways to engage your partner. So, renew your covenant as often as possible. When you can't, still express your love for each other through other means.

Don't be hindered by positions. The missionary position is not the only "Christian" position. However whatever position you want to try out, make sure your spouse is comfortable with it. Do not attempt to coerce your spouse to participate in something that makes him/her uneasy. Feel free to experiment. But be sensitive and understanding.

Sex is meant for marriage (between one man and one woman). God designed sex for the purpose of pleasure, procreation, and intimacy. His original intent was that sex would create a holy soul tie between husband and wife. Satan intends to pervert it. The following is a list of behaviors that couples should not participate in. This list is not exhaustive. If you have questions about sexual behaviors, seek godly counsel.

Unacceptable in Christian Sex

Bestiality (sex with animals)
Homosexuality/lesbianism
Incest
Masochism/Sadism (sexual pleasure from humiliation, physical or verbal abuse)
Masturbation (bringing one's self to sexual pleasure)
Necrophilia (obsession with or erotic interest in corpses)
Pornography/Sexual Images
Prostitution
Sodomy (anal sex)
Swinging (bringing in other people)
Voyeurism (watching other people have sex or watching their bodies)

These types of actions do not respect God's Word. They also dishonor your spouse. So keep your marriage bed pure and thank God every time you come together.

God wants you to fully enjoy the sexual experience. It was His idea. So relax and enjoy one another. Have fun. Connect intimately with your spouse and you will find becoming one physically, a whole lot easier.

Break Out: Husband

1. How would you rate your sex life on a scale of 1 to 10, with 10 being the best?

1 2 3 4 5 6 7 8 9 10

2. How often do you want to have sex?
3. Are you considerate of your wife in the bedroom?
4. How could you improve in relating to your wife sexually?
5. Do you struggle with pornography or sexual images in your mind?
6. Are you open to an unexpected pregnancy?
7. Do you take the time to engage your wife in foreplay?

Main Points to Consider _____

_____

_____

_____

_____

_____

_____

_____

_____

Break Out: Wife

1. How would you rate your sex life on a scale of 1 to 10, with 10 being the best?

1 2 3 4 5 6 7 8 9 10

2. How often do you want to have sex?
3. Are you considerate of your husband in the bedroom?
4. How could you improve in relating to your husband sexually?
5. Do you struggle with pornography or sexual images in your mind?
6. Are you open to an unexpected pregnancy?
7. Do you generally set the atmosphere in your bedroom for sex?

Main Points to Consider _____

_____

_____

_____

_____

_____

_____

_____

Chapter 11
Ever After

Couples often get caught up in the initial romance of the courtship and lose the excitement, shortly thereafter. Somewhere after "I Do", the sizzle is gone. And they no longer have the scent of the newlywed. The vitality has been bled out of the union. And neither spouse is the wiser on how they got here.

The thief comes ONLY to steal, kill, and destroy. He comes for no other purpose. He hates marriages. Marriage is a picture of Christ and the church (his bride) Ephesians 5:32. Satan wants to devastate that image on the earth.

And so it is, the attack on marriages begins at the altar. He works to divide. Strife, debate, unforgiveness, deceitfulness, control and manipulation are all tools in his bag. The Bible tells us that we are not ignorant of the enemy's devices. We know that this is an area, he works to defeat us. But it doesn't have to be that way. We are more than conquerors through him that loved us. We are overcomers.

Marriages don't have to dry up or die. If we wise up, we can have a vibrant, harmonious relationship that is full of power and passion. In fact, that is the heartbeat of God for all of us.

I know the thoughts that I think towards you, saith the Lord, thoughts of peace, and not of evil, to give you a hope and a future. Jeremiah 29:11

He gives us richly all things to enjoy. I Timothy 6:17b

I am come that they might have life and that they might have it more abundantly. John 10:10b

Let thy fountain be blessed: and rejoice with the wife of thy youth. Proverbs 5:18

God wants us to enjoy married life. It is the will of God that our marriages prosper.

Beloved, I wish above all things that thou mayest prosper and be in good health, even as thy soul prospereth. III John 1:2

The soul prospering has to do with a person's spiritual health. We cannot violate the principles of His Word and expect that our marriages will prosper. It's the Word of God that gives life. As we apply the Word, we will see our marriages spring alive.

We have been married nearly 29 years. We pray together and study the Word, regularly. We still have date night every Friday. (We move it around when we have to minister). We do not let the sun go do on our anger. (Yes, we still get angry with each other). And there are many issues to hammer out. So we talk them through in our husband-wife meetings. We forgive quickly. We respect and honor each other. We have made a choice to enjoy this life. We know that comes through following God's lead. He loves His bride like no other. And that is our aim – to copy Him.
We try to out-serve one another. Our idea is to spoil one

another for anyone else. We aim to be the best spouses either of us will ever have. So if one of us passes from this life, the other will know that we could never have been more fulfilled and more loved (on this earth). We are giving each other the best that we've got - now. And we are enjoying the journey. It's been fun and exciting. And there is so much more to come. We love being married. We know that God's Word works. And so we continue to work the Word.

It's sad that couples put on these spectacular weddings and then just a few short months later, they are headed to the divorce courts. The blessed "event" was intended to be a blessed "lifetime". But the two never became one.

Divorce is a violent, destructive weapon wielded against the people of God. That's why the Lord hates it so much.

Malachi 2:16 For the Lord, the God of Israel, saith that he hateth the putting away: For one covereth violence with his garment, saith the Lord of hosts, therefore take heed to your spirit, that ye deal not treacherously.

There is so much at stake. So much to lose. Often spouses are only interested in themselves when venturing down the road to divorce. They try to undo the life they've made. How do you unscramble eggs? It's just not possible. Your life is forever affected. There is no delete button. You can't undo what's been done. Divorce just makes it all messier.

Divorce tears the soul. And left in the aftermath are the children, wounded and humiliated; many taking the blame on themselves. Divorce hurts. We should not be willing to put our children through such horrendous pain.
The statistics are harrowing:

Larry Bilotta of Life Discoveries collected the damaging statistics from many sources: the children of divorced parents are twice as likely to attempt suicide, and to drop out of school. They are raped and abused more often than children of intact families. They also have more babies out of wedlock. These children are at a greater risk for many illnesses. Studies showed that even 6 years following a divorce, these children still suffered with low self-image, fear, and loneliness. They were also anxious and unhappy. They are 4 times more likely to have problems dealing with friends and peers. Half of all American children will witness the breakup of a parent's marriage. Of these, close to half will also see the breakup of a parent's second marriage. Among the millions of children who have seen their parents' divorce, one of every 10 will also live through **three or more** parental marriage breakups.

Are we even paying attention to what we are doing to ourselves more less to our children?

We must purpose in our hearts that divorce is not an option for us. We will not be covenant breakers. We must be fully committed to receiving the blessings of God in our relationships. That requires that we do **EVERYTHING** in our power to make the marriage work. It is the commitment to live joyfully ever after.

Through this handbook, we hope to have equipped you with many tools to help you build a successful relationship. Fight for your marriage. The devil is coming after your relationship. Don't just let him snatch it from you. If you need outside help, seek it.

You may find yourself so far away from those first sparks. You may be shocked at the actions and words that come from yourself and your one flesh partner. Be clear, Satan is your real enemy. He is continuously plotting against your marriage. He doesn't want it to work. Our Faithful Lord not only wants it to work, but thrive. He wants to see you two laughing, holding hands and loving on one another. Will you agree with God? Pray for your marriage. Speak words of life over your spouse.

Work to make it work.

A healthy marriage is made intentionally, through good times and not so good times.

God intended for us to have an amazing adventure in this vehicle called marriage. So let's purpose to enjoy the ride.

Break Out: Husband

1. Are you committed to making your marriage last a lifetime?
2. How does God feel about Covenant breakers?
3. Does divorce run in your family? If so, how has it hurt your family?
4. Read Joshua 9. What does it say about covenant?

Main Points to Consider _____

_____

_____

_____

_____

_____

_____

_____

_____

_____

_____

Break Out: Wife

1. Are you committed to making your marriage last a lifetime?
2. How does God feel about Covenant breakers?
3. Does divorce run in your family? If so, how has it hurt your family?
4. Read Joshua 9. What does it say about covenant?

Main Points to Consider _____

_____

_____

_____

_____

_____

_____

_____

_____

_____

_____

_____

Notes:

10 Commandments of Marriage

I
Thou shall keep God first in your relationship.
Thou shalt have no other gods before me. Exodus 20:3

II
Thou shalt pray together for each other and for your relationship.
Again I say unto you, that if two of you shall agree on earth as touching anything that they shall ask, it shall be done for them of my Father which is in heaven. Matt 18:19

III
Thou shall put thy spouse before all others.
For this cause shall a man leave his father and mother and be joined unto his wife, and they two shall be one flesh. Eph. 5:31

IV
Thou shall not go to bed angry.
Be ye angry, and sin not; let not the sun go down upon your wrath. Eph. 4:26

V
Thou shall speak life to your marriage and spouse.
Let no corrupt communication proceed out of your mouth, but that which is good to the use of edifying. Eph. 4:29

VI
Thou shall forgive quickly.
If he trespass against the seven times in a day and seven times in a day turn again to thee, saying I repent; thou shalt forgive Luke 17:4

VII
Thou shall not withhold sex from each other.
Defraud ye not one the other except it be with consent for a time, that you may give yourselves to fasting and prayer; and come together again, that satan tempt you not for your incontinency. I Cori. 7:5

VIII
Thou shall submit to each other.
Submit yourselves one to another in the fear of God. Eph. 5:21

IX
Thou shall date thy mate.
Let thy fountain be blessed, rejoice with the wife of thy youth. Prov.5:16

X
Thou shall talk to your spouse.
Come now and let us reason together. Isaiah 1:18a

Newlywed
Q&A's

Newlywed Q&A's

1. We are newly married. I have 2 children from a previous relationship. My children are five and seven years old. They are the main reason we argue. I love my husband, but I am not sure he knows how to discipline children. He loves my children but he thinks they should have chores. I don't mind cleaning behind them. Besides, I think that my children are too young for chores. He often wants to put them on a punishment for small things. We do not agree at all. My husband likes order. I understand that you cannot always have order in a house with small children. I think he is just too hard on them.

→Children should be handled with an even hand. That means they need to experience love and gentleness along with discipline and correction. Even the smallest child needs correction. A two-year-old needs to learn that he cannot have his way. Your children can and should be taught to clean up behind themselves and do other age-appropriate chores. Your house doesn't have to be picture perfect. But you can have order. You both need to compromise in some areas of child-rearing. Talk to an impartial party or seek Christian counseling.

2. Should we attend the same church?

→Absolutely! We **strongly** believe that couples should worship together. Oneness should be present in every area of the relationship. Pray about the place of worship that the Lord is leading you and attend together.

3. Where should we spend holidays?

→It can be complex sometimes. With divorce more prevalent, there are now more than 2 families in which to split the celebrations. Couples now have to choose between husband's mom and her husband and husband's dad's and his wife. And the wife has two families as well. Sit down and discuss your options. A lot of couples alternate between the families. Her family will get Christmas. His family will get Thanksgiving. Other couples keep Christmas Day for themselves, and spend the days before celebrating with family. For example, Dec 23 is spent with her family. And Dec 24th is spent with his. It's important to leave room for your own celebrations. So that you can create some traditions of your own.

4. Should we live in an apartment or house?

→New couples usually want to start their new life in a new house. The reality is that most are not prepared for owning a new home. The upkeep of a new home, mortgage payment, taxes and insurance are usually more than a newlywed couple can handle. It is best to save up before taking on such a big task in your first years of marriage. Once your financial ducks are in a row, save up a healthy down payment. And when you feel you can allocate 25% of your net income towards a mortgage payment without feeling a pinch, then you may be ready. If you do it too soon, you could be subjecting your marriage to unnecessary stress.

5. My mother-in-law doesn't like me. She pretends she does when my husband is around. But I can feel it in her actions. How do I handle it?

→The in-law issue is not an uncommon one. Many parents have a hard time letting go of their children when they get married. Keep your husband aware of what your concerns are. Do not confront her on the issue. When there is a manifested attack, allow your husband to confront her. However, try to reassure her that she is an important part of your life. Spend time with her. Do kind deeds for her. Try to understand the loss she feels. Pray for her. Also pray for your husband to see what needs to be seen. And pray that he has the courage to lovingly confront his mother (if necessary).

6. My stepchildren's mother is very jealous hearted. She seems to be always trying to sabotage my relationship with my husband. She teaches her children to talk back to me. I believe she wants my husband back. She dresses provocatively around him. He thinks I am overreacting.

→Your husband needs to take your concerns seriously. Bring this issue to the husband-wife meeting. Even if it's not true, it is important that he hears you. This makes you uncomfortable, so he needs to be sensitive to your feelings. Set precautions around your relationship to keep out her influence. For instance, your husband should not allow his children to talk back to you. He should also avoid face to face interaction with his children's mother (as much as possible). Your husband's sensitivity and wisdom can keep this issue from escalating. But he must hear you.

7. My best friend is a guy that I have known for more than 10 years. My husband (1 year) doesn't have a problem with our relationship. But my mom said it is wrong. Am I supposed to just cut my best friend off after all these years?

→Your husband should be your very best friend. There is an intimacy that husband and wife should share that cannot include anyone else. The scriptures clearly say that we should leave others and cleave to our spouses. No, you don't have to cut your friend off, but the relationship needs to adjust. Allow room for your marriage to grow. You must become one with your husband. The marriage must take priority over all other relationships. If this guy is a good friend, then he should understand.

8. My wife wants me to use condoms when we are sexually intimate, because she doesn't want to use any other birth control. She thinks the other methods have too many side effects. I don't want to use condoms. What should we do?

→You would need to decide which is more important and in what order: (1) avoiding pregnancy (2) your sexual pleasure (3) your wife's health. Once you've ordered these priorities, the two of you need to sit down and talk with a health professional about your options in birth control. Then you can make the decision that is right for you both.

9. How often should a husband and wife come together sexually?

→Couples should come together regularly. There is no magic number. Each couple is different and has different desires. There are also varying seasons of the marriage relationship. A woman may have given birth or may be experiencing menopause. Health issues can cause hindrances on both sides. There are a lot of dynamics that affect the sexual relationship. The best advice is to come together as often as possible.

10. Is it wrong for a wife to work outside of the home?

→The scriptures do not give us that impression. It does let us know that the home should be her priority. Titus 2:4-5 tells us that the elder women should teach the young women how to love her husband, her children, be responsible, discreet, chaste, and to *be keepers of the home*. So her primary responsibility is to tend to the home. The husband's primary responsibility is to provide for his family. The choice to work outside of the home is that of the wife and her husband. However if she does work outside of the home, the husband should participate in the maintenance of the household.

11. How soon should we start a family?

→It is ideal to wait at least a year to get to know each other as husband and wife. However, it is more important that the two of you agree on the timing.

12. My wife has enormous student debt accrued before we married. I am a strong money manager and have very little debt. Should we keep our money separate and each pay down our loans, or should we combine our debt and pay it together.

→When you take the vow to marry someone, you merge everything, debt and assets. If she had millions of dollars in assets, there would be no question about integrating the finances. You are working to become one. The best idea is to merge all of your accounts and pay the loans as one.

13. My niece is 21 years old. I have been like a mother to her since her mom, my sister, died when she was 2. She is a good girl and she works hard. I have been giving her $400 a month toward her expenses up until we got married. My husband is against me helping her pay bills. What should I do?

→Follow your husband. It seems like you are enabling your niece. She is an adult. She needs to learn how to take care of herself. You should sit down with her and help her set up her own budget. You are hurting her by causing her to depend on you for support. Help her become self-sufficient. Giving her money every month is not a good idea. But, if she needs help once in a while, that is something you and hubby can discuss.

Notes:

Notes:

The Jones' have another published book entitled:

When the Vow Breaks currently in bookstores.

<u>Other Recommended Reading</u>:

The Case for Marriage - Linda J. Waite & Maggie Gallagher

Devotions for Couples - Patrick Morley

Help Me, I'm Married - Joyce Meyer

The Husband Handbook - Dr. Bob Moorehead

Love For A Lifetime - Dr. James Dobson

Love Must Be Tough - Dr. James Dobson

Resolving Conflict in Marriage - Darrell L. Hines

What Wives Wish Their Husbands Knew
About Women - Dr. James Dobson

About the Authors

Apostle Oscar & Prophetess Crystal Jones

have been celebrating their covenant love for nearly 29 years. Their passion for one another has yielded a great harvest. They have 5 children and one daughter in love: Jake & Keila, Kyria, Charity, LaTina, and Christopher. They also delight in their 4 precious grandchildren: Kristin D'Ashley, Arielle Joy, Jaiman Allen, and Elijah Christopher.

Oscar & Crystal are both teachers by trade. They have taught in both the private and public sectors. Oscar has taught for both Detroit Public Schools and Oakland Unified Schools. He has recently left teaching after 27 years to pursue fulltime ministry. Prophetess Crystal is a licensed and practicing realtor for Century 21 Professional Realty.

Pastors Oscar & Crystal have an apostolic and prophetic mandate. They oversee **Greater Works Family Ministries** in Detroit, MI**, Marriage For A Lifetime Ministries** in Detroit, MI. They are founders of **Agape International Association of Churches and Para-churches** and **Alive Christian Fellowship** of Oakland, California. They are serious about kingdom building.

The couple has hosted a weekly call-in radio broadcast called **Grounds For Marriage** where they discussed issues relevant to marriage and the family.

They have also been featured guests on several radio and television broadcasts.

The couple has co-authored a book entitled, **"When The Vow Breaks"** which is now in its second printing. They aspire to leave a legacy of hope and healing to marriages all over the world.

These long-time honeymooners continue to have a passion for marriage ministry. They have a unique team ministry where they speak together as one voice. They are in demand as conference speakers.

To book them at your conference you may write to:

Marriage For A Lifetime Ministries

Your testimonies and prayer requests are also welcome

P.O. Box 24906
Oakland, CA 94623

Or

P.O. Box 19774
Detroit, MI 48219

1.888.884.3556
Email: jones@marriage4alifetime.org

Please visit their website at

www.marriage4alifetime.org

Other books available through:

Destiny House Publishing
www.destinyhousepublishing.com

No Longer A Dream
A Step-By-Step Guide to Writing Your First Book

By Crystal A. Jones
ISBN 1452828334

You have dreams in your heart of becoming an accomplished author, but you don't know where to start. Your dreams are just a few pages away. No Longer A Dream will take you step by step through the process of completing your first manuscript.

10 Steps to Entrepreneurship

By Rochelle Smith
ISBN 1451539509

Have you ever thought about starting a business? But you weren't sure where to start? This easy to read guide will help you get that business off the ground.

Barren, but Pregnant with Purpose

Victory in Your Defeat

By Joceline Bronson
ISBN 1442187271

God says in this book, that you too can have victory in the
midst of defeat. Right now, you might see the defeat, death,
distress and the barrenness of your womb. But just know that
on the inside of these pages are words
that will provoke the promise.

**Discover How You Can Restore
Hope & Healing In Your Marriage**

**By Oscar & Crystal Jones
ISBN 145054214X**

Marriage is a sacred union in the eyes of God. Yet, marriage are failing everyday. What is the standard? What should the Christian response be when sin invades the union? Is divorce the only option when there is a breach?
Get these answers and more.